The Best Day

by Heather Hill
illustrated by Ann Iosa

Today is the best day of the whole
summer! It is a birthday party for
America. My town throws the biggest
party around. It is really fun; no one is
disappointed.

The team began planning the party last summer. It takes a long time to prepare for a big party. How many floats, clowns, and balloons will we need? How many hot dogs should we order?

I woke up at the crack of dawn! Mom said, "Don't wake your sisters up." I didn't want them to miss out on the fun. I blew my horn until they woke up. They're a little grumpy.

4

This party is really exciting because my dad is the Grand Marshall. He will ride in the first red car. The mayor and our state senator will follow him. We are very proud of Dad!

We drop Dad at the school statue. The floats are lining up. The judges will take a good look at each float and then vote for the best. Which one will be the funniest?

6

We found a perfect spot to sit right
in the middle. We will grab the treats
that the clowns throw. We will wave
to the folks on floats and to the Grand
Marshall, Dad.

After the floats, trucks, and bands pass
by, we meet at the park. We have
the biggest picnic and baseball game
of the summer. Last, we look at the
beautiful fireworks in the sky.

8